Turning Your Tech Hobbies Into a Career™

GETTING PAID TO
Blog and Vlog

RICHARD BARRINGTON

ROSEN
PUBLISHING®

New York

Published in 2017 by The Rosen Publishing Group, Inc.
29 East 21st Street, New York, NY 10010

First Edition

Library of Congress Cataloging-in-Publication Data

Names: Barrington, Richard, 1961– author.
Title: Getting paid to blog and vlog / Richard Barrington.
Description: First edition. | New York : Rosen Publishing, 2017 | Series:
  Turning your tech hobbies into a career | Includes bibliographical
  references and index.
Identifiers: LCCN 2016017410 | ISBN 9781508172901 (library bound)
Subjects: LCSH: Blogs—Vocational guidance—Juvenile literature. | Video
  blogs—Vocational guidance—Juvenile literature.
Classification: LCC TK5105.8884 B37 2017 | DDC 302.23/14023—dc23
LC record available at https://lccn.loc.gov/2016017410

Manufactured in Malaysia

Contents

Introduction

People often dream of making a living doing something they really love—whether it is sports, fashion, the entertainment business, or helping others. In the early part of the twenty-first century, blogging, either in writing or on video, has allowed people to turn those interests into a career by writing, talking about, or demonstrating tips on such topics. Some bloggers have become online celebrities themselves doing just that.

An exciting thing about blogging is that it has made popular media more democratic. It used to be that a relatively small number of television networks, radio stations, and publications determined who got a platform for expressing themselves. Now, it is an age of do-it-yourself media. The equipment needed for blogging is minimal and often found in ordinary households and schools. There are few barriers to getting started.

That ease of entry is a good thing about blogging, but it is also part of its curse. There are now a great many voices competing for attention, and only a tiny minority attract a significant audience. Still, blogging has become diverse enough that there are other ways to make a living at it besides creating a hit blog. Businesses use blogging as a way of keeping their products in front of people in a fresh way. Specialized websites use blogging as a way of giving detailed advice on a variety of subjects, from finances to social issues.

Mode Media (formerly Glam Media) demonstrates how blogging creates a brand based on a common interest and expertise to share with an online audience.

Beyond the profit potential of blogging, another important aspect of it is its role is in building communities. It helps people with similar interests to find each other and discuss topics that don't get much coverage in mainstream media. Barriers of geography are broken down, and people from all kinds of backgrounds can freely exchange opinions, advice, or jokes with others whose tastes match their own.

Another great thing about blogging is that while youth can be a disadvantage in most occupations, it is very much a positive for bloggers. Teens and young adults today are often more comfortable using technology than their parents. They are up on the latest trends in social media, and they have the fresh perspective that is the essence of blogging. So, whether a person is in it to make a buck or just to feel part of a community, it is pretty much never too early to start blogging.

This book will describe some of the basics needed to get started, including the typical elements that make up a blog and some tips on managing the content. It will also describe some methods of building an audience, and the various ways bloggers can cash in on their popularity or otherwise make a living by blogging.

Finally, this book will discuss some of the trends that are shaping where blogging is going, because it is a fast-changing field. Types of content, communication style, and business models for blogs are evolving rapidly. It is entirely possible that somebody reading this book today will be helping to shape the future of blogging in a year's time.

Chapter ONE

DIY Media Is the New Normal

So what exactly is a blog?

The answer to that question is tough to pin down. The nature of blogging is changing all the time, and very diverse forms have already evolved. However, there are some defining characteristics that are common to most blogs.

The word "blog" is a contraction of the term "web log." A log is akin to a diary, but it is often focused on a particular subject or pursuit rather than being purely an expression of personal thoughts and feelings. "Vlog" is a contraction of the term "video log," and it is a type of blog that is in video rather than written form.

More than anything, what has defined blogging is its do-it-yourself nature. Blogs tend to have an informal feel to them, and it does not require much technical expertise or expense to get started. The fact that blogging is so easily done has allowed hundreds of thousands of fresh new voices to emerge. Most don't have massive audiences, but without blogging their ideas might never find any platform.

Success and Mortality

A successful blog can be hugely popular. Each of the top fifteen blogs is estimated to draw an audience of at least ten million people a month. Sites like the Huffington Post and TMZ have moved way beyond niche markets, and now are every bit as visible as traditional mainstream media outlets.

Blogging can not only make websites popular, but it can turn bloggers into celebrities. Tavi Gevinson, who started the blog Style Rookie as an eleven-year-old, became an internationally respected fashion expert by the time she was in her tweens. Gevinson was a late bloomer compared to the star of EvanTubeHD, who at seven years old attracted enough of a following reviewing toys on YouTube that his channel's earnings are estimated to be in the hundreds of thousands of dollars.

Whether a person values fame, fortune, or just reaching out to other people, blogging has the potential to attract a massive audience. This is not the norm, however. It is hard to estimate how many blogs there are, because in addition to dedicated blog sites, many people use social media outlets such as Facebook and YouTube as a platform for blogging.

Tavi Gevinson, seen here sorting through potential content for her website, turned her interest in fashion into a blogging career at an early age.

One estimate is that there are over one hundred million bloggers in the United States alone. That is roughly one-third of the US population, which does not leave much room for the average site to carve out a large audience.

As a result, many blogs soon go belly-up. The internet is a virtual graveyard of blogs that have died off, most of them unnoticed. Therefore, an important thing to keep in mind when a person starts blogging is that while it probably won't be an easy route to fame and fortune, it can still be a valuable experience in other ways.

While blogs come in a variety of formats and cover a wide range of topics, what successful ones share is that they make people want to keep coming back. To understand how they do this, a good place to start is by looking at what role blogs play, and some of the things that go into them.

THE ROLE OF BLOGS AND VLOGS

With so many different formats and subjects, one thing that defines blogs is not how they look but what role they play.

While a small minority of blogs have mass appeal, more often what blogging does is allow people to reach a niche audience. This allows a wider range of creative expression to see the light of day, and gives people access to highly-specialized

Interior design is an example of a very specialized subject that can find a wide audience through a blog

advice from people who have encountered challenges similar to their own.

Increasingly, blogs do not just represent a single voice, but rather bring together a diverse group of contributors. The value of sites like the Huffington Post, BuzzFeed, and Mashable is that they act like a museum curator or a newspaper editor: they filter out the less professional bloggers while bringing together content that is likely to interest people, and help present it in ways that get their attention.

Of course, there would not be nearly as much financial investment put into blogging if there was not a profit motive involved. An important role of blogging is to provide content that drives traffic to an e-retailer. That traffic is valuable from a business standpoint because users can view advertisements, shop, and become more familiar with a brand's products.

BUILDING PEER-TO-PEER COMMUNITIES

Socially, a key role that blogs play is to help build peer-to-peer communities. They facilitate discussion of interests and concerns common to a particular group. They provide advice, recreation, and products to their particular audience. In a sense, they are a gathering place the way town squares were one hundred years ago or shopping malls were thirty years ago.

Unlike town squares and shopping malls though, blogs do not require that the people they attract live anywhere nearby. This allows communities to form around much narrower, more specific interests, or around issues people might feel shy about discussing face to face.

Zoe Suggs has built an international following through her web blog "Zoella," at https://www.zoella.co.uk, by offering beauty, fashion, and lifestyle tips.

The ability to build peer-to-peer communities can be especially powerful for teen and young adult blogs. There aren't many mainstream outlets discussing emerging trends that are important to a young audience. And for some that do exist, young people find them unappealing because they do not want grown-ups telling them what to think and what to like. The immediacy of blogging, and the open access it grants to new contributors, is a natural vehicle for providing teens and young adults with content they find fresh and relevant.

So, whether it is a YouTube comedy channel like Smosh, a vlog on beauty tips like Zoella, or blogs dealing with more serious issues like teen pregnancy or coming to terms with sexual orientation, blogging can be instrumental in helping young people find communities that give them a sense of belonging.

BUSINESS BLOGS AND VLOGS

Examples cited so far show how blogs can be sources of entertainment and information and can also be focal points for various communities. They can also play a role in helping businesses sell their products and provide services to their customers.

Businesses are increasingly including blogs on their websites for a variety of reasons. Blogs provide an outlet for regularly updated content, which helps promote products by keeping the name in front of customers. Blogs can also help service customers by addressing concerns that have come up in the marketplace. Vlogs are an excellent tool for businesses to use to provide visual demonstrations of how their products can be used.

Some businesses sell to other businesses rather than to individual consumers. This is known as business-to-business or B2B marketing. Blogs are a great fit for B2B marketing because they are easily geared to a specialized rather than a mass audience. The mainstream media are not likely to cover information about a new type of electronic inventory system or an innovative medical device, but specialized B2B blogs can help those products reach people who have a use for them.

The challenge for a business-based blog is drawing the line between the personal informality of a blog and the carefully controlled image of a company. It is especially important for business blogs to have quality control procedures to make sure that confidential or false information is not disclosed and that the blogger does not say anything unprofessional.

INGREDIENTS OF A BLOG

Clearly, blogs can play a number of social and commercial roles, but how exactly do they do it? What elements go into a blog?

Well, there are no formal rules—after all, that is one of the points of blogging. Instead, blogging can be thought of like an old family recipe: there are some specific ingredients that are usually used, but how they are put together and prepared differs almost every single time.

Here, though, are some of the usual ingredients:

- **The right name.** It seems like a minor detail, but coming up with the right name is one of the hardest parts of any venture. Some popular blogs, like Business Insider and Tech Crunch, have names that give people an immediate idea of what they are about. Others, like Mashable and Cheezburger are more

Blogging can be done on a flexible schedule and from anywhere there is internet access, making it an excellent hobby for students.

obscure. Whether it is a descriptive name or something more whimsical, what matters is that it is memorable and relatively easy to type into a search engine or url bar.

- **Frequent posts.** The point of a blog is to keep discussions going and offer insights on things before they become old news.

- **Brevity.** People like their blogs in small, easily digestible portions. Quick reads are what they expect, so bloggers should think of around one thousand words as a maximum per post. If a blogger has more to say on a subject, it is easy to break the discussion up into multiple posts.

- **Timeline.** The classic organization for a blog is a timeline of posts listed in reverse chronological order, so the latest is always front and center. Even as blogs have taken on more dynamic formats, the general principle of "most recent = most prominent" remains the norm.

- **Category headings.** The problem with the timeline approach is that it can make it hard to locate a post on a particular topic. The solution to this is to also have a variety of subject headings along the top or side of the page, so people can click on those headings and find previous posts that center on that category.

- **Bio/about.** This should be brief and not too formal. The description of the author should match the tone and content of the blog. The idea is to describe a person users would want to listen to about the subjects covered in the blog.

- **Graphics.** The layout should not be too static. Clicking on a website and seeing just a long column of words does not usually make people eager to dive in. Each page should mix in some graphics and photos where possible.

- **Video.** Obviously, this is central to a vlog, but even a written blog should consider mixing in some video. It can show action relevant to topics being discussed and can help the audience get to know the blogger a little better.

PLATFORMS

The platforms on which blogs are launched boil down to four categories:

1. **Social media platforms.** Whether it is a video channel on YouTube or a Twitter account that is used to actively accumulate followers, posting content on social media requires minimal set-up and maintenance work. However, it also makes it harder

WordPress, at https://wordpress.com, is an online publishing platform that makes it easy for new bloggers to set up their sites and get started.

to establish a distinct identity as a blogger and can restrict the distinctive content and profit potential of the blog.

2. **Blog hosting platforms.** Ready-made blogging services like Tumblr and WordPress provide tools that make it easy to set up and customize a blog with its own distinctive look and content. However, the web address will still be a subset of the blogging services address, which carries less weight with search engines and implies the blog is not a professional, long-term effort.

3. **Aggregators.** Sites like LifeHacker are not built around a single voice, but bring together quality posts from a variety of bloggers. A blogger may have to build up a track record to get on one of these aggregator sites, but when this happens it is like a stamp of approval for the blogger and a quick way to reach a wider audience.

4. **Self-hosting.** Starting a blog with its own stand-alone url and computer server requires the most effort and technical skill. However, it also provides the most control over the content and business model.

Blogging on a social media site is an easy way to get started. With virtually no upfront effort, it allows newbies to see if they can sustain the effort of generating content and whether they can start to build an audience. After a while, though, it makes sense to try to work up the ladder to either own a proprietary url or to earn a place on an aggregator site that will help the blog reach a wider audience.

Chapter TWO

Learning to Blog

As popular as blogging has become, accredited courses in blogging, let alone degrees, are still hard to find. In part, this may be because putting together a good blog does not rely on just a single academic discipline, but rather a range of diverse skills.

Even for those who specialize in one aspect of blogging, recognizing the other skills involved and trying to understand the rudiments of each one will make a person a better blogger.

Despite the do-it-yourself ethos of blogging, doing it well requires developing some skill sets. Coursework in any of the areas discussed below could be useful in pursuing blogging as a career.

TECHNOLOGICAL SKILLS

For those who want the most control over how their blogs look and function, it helps to learn something about the following technical areas:

- **HTML.** This stands for hypertext mark-up language, and it is a form of computer code that describes how online text should be formatted. It inserts instructions into the text as to when to bold, underline, insert, replace, or otherwise manipulate the way

While there are no formal requirements for blogging, learning some basic technical and design skills can make it easier to create eye-catching posts.

content will appear to the user. Even for those bloggers who do not intend to rely on their own technical savvy, an introductory course in HTML and other online computer coding basics can help a blogger understand the potential for how a site can be set up and how to communicate better with technical people.

- **Layout and design.** Even for people who are not visually oriented—or perhaps especially for them—coursework in layout and design can help them appreciate how the way material is set up on a page affects the way people read it.

Coding is the key to a highly functional blog, whether it's a template supplied by a blogging website or a custom-made webpage.

- **Graphic design.** While layout determines how material is arranged on a page, graphic design involves creating individual visuals on the page. These can be charts, infographics, picture mash-ups, etc. Visuals that look amateurish can undermine the credibility of a site's content. Fortunately, a wide variety of graphic packages, such as CorelDraw and a variety of offerings from Adobe (including the popular Photoshop), can help polish those images. An introductory course in graphic design can help a blogger learn what software is out there and decide what would be most useful for the situation.

Writer, Computer Whiz, or Salesperson: What is a Blogger, Really?

Looking at the diverse disciplines that are involved in blogging raises the question: Which skill set really defines a blogger? Are they primarily writers, or is technical savvy more important? Is the real talent in promoting and capitalizing on the blog?

The answer is probably all and none of the above. Technical, communication, and business skills all play a role in a blog's success, but there are two primary things that define a good blogger:

1. **Having something worthwhile to say.** Face it, there will be no shortage of other bloggers commenting on last night's big game or the latest celebrity sighting. To attract and keep an audience, a blogger needs to have something special to say. That something special might come from detailed subject knowledge, it might come from a talent for an especially insightful turn of phrase, or it might simply be a function of an engaging personality that translates well to blog posts or videos. Whatever it is, this kind of differing perspective is what makes a blog special.

(continued on the next page)

(continued from the previous page)

2. **Knowing how to put the pieces together.** No one expects any one person to be, say, an expert on the hip-hop scene and have the technical savvy to create a sharp-looking website and write well and be able to promote the blog to popularity. Each person should decide which elements of blogging success he or she is good at, and then find other experts or services to fill in the missing pieces.

- **Server set-up and support.** Bloggers who want to host their own sites will need sufficient computer network skills to set up and support their own computer server. The server provides the computing power necessary for the site and helps direct users to and around the site. Coursework in computer hardware and networking would be helpful for understanding these functions.

COMMUNICATION SKILLS

Blogs generally use multiple communication elements to get their messages across and engage users. The following are some fields a would-be blogger should consider studying to hone the necessary skills:

- **Writing.** A good blog relies on compelling writing. Even vlogs should be scripted enough for the content to be tightly organized and run within a targeted timeframe. Polishing up on the fundamentals of writing, as mundane as it might be, is

Learning a range of communication skills and how to work with multiple types of media helps enhance and expand blogging abilities.

a good starting point. Nothing undermines a message more quickly than childish mistakes in grammar and spelling. Courses in essay and creative writing are also worth considering. Blogs often seek to present evidence to make a specific point, and experience with essay writing can help sharpen this approach. A creative writing background can add the story-telling elements that help make posts more entertaining.

- **Journalism.** This might seem like an extension of writing, but journalism is a distinct discipline in itself. Studying journalism can help a blogger develop investigative skills, learn how to produce well-written stories quickly, present information in a newsworthy manner, and understand some of the basic legal concerns involved with commenting publicly on other people and companies.

- **Personal presentation.** For those planning to vlog, some coursework on public speaking or video presentation might be helpful. These teach people to understand how to control their voices, facial expressions, and body language to present a clear and believable message. Studying video presentation can also help a vlogger understand camera setup, lighting, and audio recording. Cameras, lighting, and sound equipment are all

Adding video presentations should not require a great deal of expensive equipment, but it can give a blog a more dynamic appearance.

expensive, so taking some courses could be a good investment for knowing what to buy.

- **Multimedia presentation.** A written blog and a vlog is not an either/or choice. A dynamic blog might employ both, plus other visual aids besides video. Coursework in multimedia presentation can teach a person how to combine words, graphics, and video to make the content come alive.

BUSINESS SKILLS

Most people think of bloggers more as entertainers or journalists than as businesspeople, but for those who want to attract an audience and possibly make some money in the process, some business skills come into play.

More on developing a blog as a business will be described in chapter 4, but in terms of acquiring the right skills to do this, here are some areas of coursework worth considering:

- **Promotion.** This might include public relations or marketing. Relevant coursework should have an emphasis on digital media promotion and not just on traditional press outreach. Ideally, a blog would be strong enough to build an audience by word-of-mouth, but internet buzz is not usually generated by accident. For example, a video going viral might seem like a natural occurrence—after all, the expression "going viral" suggests it catches on naturally, like a virus spreading. In actuality, there is a good chance that it was the result of a carefully orchestrated promotional campaign using social media, networks of other bloggers, and other techniques.

The Importance of Site Housekeeping

Whether you choose to focus on learning the technical, communications, or business side of blogging, when you first start out it might seem that the primary challenge is producing new content. While this task never goes away, another challenge soon joins it: site housekeeping.

This is a little bit like cleaning up a bedroom. From day to day, it is easy to let things slide. However, if things continue to be tossed around and left there, it becomes hard for people to find what they want. Pretty soon, the place is an eyesore that no one wants to go near.

Similarly, old content on blogs has to be cleaned up on occasion. Posts that may have lasting relevance should be organized into category pages so they can be easily accessed even after they have slipped a ways down the timeline.

It is important to distinguish between evergreen content, which has that kind of lasting relevance, and short-term content which is relevant when written but has references or information that quickly become dated. Out-of-date content should be culled from the site periodically, especially if it essentially covers the same ground as more up-to-date posts.

In short, a good blogger has to not only learn how to create new content, but how to maintain existing content. Cleaning up out-of-date content makes sure that visitors searching the blog will not come across a four-year-old post that makes the site seem out of touch. The clutter of dated material is like a pile of dirty socks on the bedroom floor—

- **eCommerce.** This involves the process of selling things over the internet and also of capitalizing on a website or channel's audience. The expression that is often used for figuring out how to profit from online material is "monetizing content." Successful blogs often follow the approach of building an audience first and figuring out how to monetize later, but knowing what some of the options are from the start will help a blogger lay the groundwork for profitability. The field of ecommerce and,

BuzzFeed, at https://www.buzzfeed.com, is an example of how being on top of breaking news can help a site reach a wider audience as certain stories go viral.

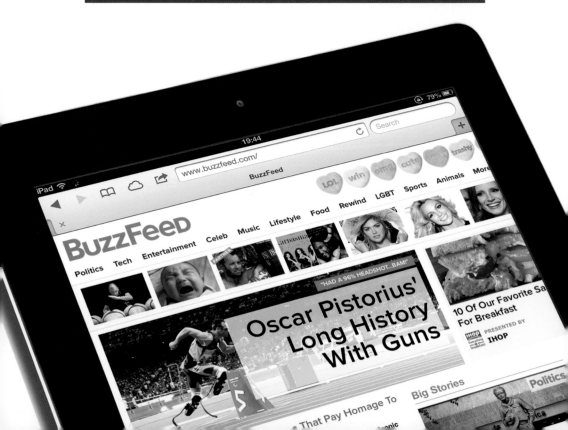

in particular, of monetizing content is developing so quickly that any coursework on the subject has to focus on the latest developments in order to be relevant.

- **Search engine optimization (SEO).** This is the practice of producing content that will rank well in online searches on related topics. SEO makes online writing a little different from other forms of writing. It requires telling a good story while also incorporating the elements that search engine algorithms will look for in ranking search results. As those algorithms are being adjusted frequently, this is another area of study that needs to be absolutely up-to-date to be useful.

- **Social media marketing.** This is yet another fast-developing aspect of the business of blogging. Whether a blog is based on a social media platform or simply uses social media to promote its posts, learning about social media marketing could help with finding a wider audience.

Chapter THREE

Keys to Being a Successful Blogger or Vlogger

As noted in chapter 1, the basic components of a blog are fairly simple, and it is easy to get started. Chapter 2 described some areas of study that can help give a person a good background for blogging. Once a blogger is ready to jump in and get started, how do they become successful? What is it that makes some blogs wildly popular, while most fail to attract an audience beyond a few friends and family members?

This chapter will look at some of the keys to having a successful blog.

THE MESSAGE

For all of the attitude, design elements, and technological enhancements that go into a blog, the message is the meat of it (unless it is a vegan blog, in which case the message is some

Sports, and especially a focus on a specific team or even a specific player, can be a good focal point for a blog's content.

other kind of protein). A new blogger needs to figure out why people will come to the site and why they will want to come back and also tell their friends about it.

A good way to focus the message is to clarify what the blog's mission is. The natural instinct for many people is to talk about anything and everything that comes to mind, but unless people already know who you are, such an undefined mission makes it difficult for people to understand why they should want to pay attention in the first place.

Is it the Message or the Messenger that Makes a Blog?

Thinking about how a blog's message helps define the blog raises the question of whether it is the message itself or who is delivering the message that is the key to a blog's popularity.

It can be either one. Take two very different examples. The name Ken Pomeroy is only familiar to very ardent sports fans, yet his site, kenpom.com, has built such a reputation that it is often quoted by big-time, mainstream publications like *Sports Illustrated*. This is despite the fact that kenpom.com is intentionally short on personality. It hits a visitor in the face with a page full of statistics right off the bat, and then keeps the stats coming.

The niche kenpom.com has captured is an audience of people who cannot get enough of sophisticated statistics on college basketball. For anyone wondering just how big a niche that is, just look around a typical office during the NCAA basketball tournament. During March Madness, at least, college basketball stats are a highly in-demand commodity.

The point is, given its numbers-rather-than-commentary approach to sports, with kenpom.com it is clearly the message rather than the messenger that makes the blog.

Contrast that with PerezHilton.com. From the famous family name to the breathless dishing on celebrity gossip, the idea here is that this is a place where ordinary folks can go to have a Hollywood insider let them in on a few secrets. It is doubtful that anything on PerezHilton.com will be remembered beyond the next movie premiere, but in the meantime, an estimated 14.5 million monthly visitors are checking out what Perez has to say. In this case, the messenger rather than the message is what makes the blog.

Examples of how a blog could define its mission might be things like, "This blog will help casual baseball fans understand how advanced baseball metrics apply to what they see when they watch a game," or "These posts will center around simple fashion hacks for people who don't want to spend a lot of time and money on how they look."

It helps to distinguish a blog if it caters to a distinct niche, but no matter how specialized, with millions of blogs out there the mission alone cannot be expected to make a blog stand out. What also defines a blog is how distinct a voice it presents. That voice may be supportive or snarky, analytical or charmingly scatterbrained, but it should give the blog a personality that can stand out from other voices talking about the same subject.

Beyond knowing what to say and having an engaging way of saying it, a blog can gain an audience by dealing with subjects that are on people's minds. That does not mean having to jump on every cultural bandwagon that comes along. A blogger may want to be known for having a finger on the popular pulse, or for giving pop culture the finger. But, whether a blogger is a cheerleader or a critic of what's hot, it is important to be thoroughly plugged into what the audience is watching, reading, and discussing.

PRESENTATION

The way information is presented is increasingly important to a blog's success. The do-it-yourself spirit still lives in that the tools to put together eye-catching layouts, easy-to-digest-graphics, and video content are readily available. A serious blogger today had better figure out how to use those tools to make the site look like a serious player.

After all, the average person does not have the stamina to wade through long blocks of text. Blogs come alive when they combine words and pictures to tell a story, via charts, slideshows, and infographics.

Also the visual style of a site should reinforce the nature of the blog. Curvy letters and splashes of pink and purple would be right for a site dedicated to preteen heartthrobs; for a hard-headed economics blog, not so much.

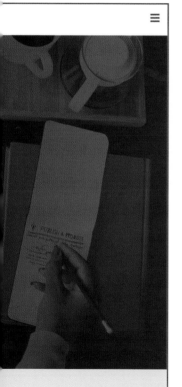

Along with being consistent with the nature of the blog, the look of the site should also be differentiated in some way. Ideally, one glance should be enough to tell a visitor whose site they are looking at.

More and more, video is an important element in how a blog presents its content. This goes without saying for vlogs, but even traditional word-based blogs are finding it important to spice up their text with a few video clips. Those who have taken the step of becoming proficient at video editing can add further life to the presentation by switching between different camera angles or cutting in multiple commenters.

Blogging platforms give a ready means for launching a blog, but a key to success is the creativity the blogger brings to the content and its presentation.

Digital Footprint

When contemplating their message and presentation, bloggers are naturally focused on the here-and-now: how to get their target audience to pay attention to today's post. However, it would also be wise to give some thought to a different, future audience.

Everything posted online has the potential to create a permanent digital footprint. So, a blogger must understand that it is not just today's target audience that will read his opinions or watch her escapades. Some colleges may research an applicant's digital footprint, as might potential employers. There are even sites that help visitors research the online history of people they are dating.

Beyond that, there is the scariest unintended audience of all: someday, a blogger's kids might see today's post.

It might take some of the spice out of a blog to have to clean up some of the details of a funny drinking story, or pull some punches in a vehement political commentary. Independent bloggers have the advantage of being their own censors, but this is also a responsibility. When exercising that responsibility, it is wise to think about the type of digital footprint you are leaving.

Cell phones, iPads, and other technology allow bloggers to develop content and post from just about anywhere. But taking the time to refine a post makes for better content.

SPECIALIZED KNOWLEDGE

If crafting a distinct message and presenting it well are keys to a successful blog, how does one decide what that message should be? A good place to start is with personal knowledge and interests.

For example, a great way for teens to get started in blogging is by focusing on issues that are important to themselves and their peers. For example, in her early teens Callie Reiff turned her interest in style into a blogging career. Her site, Callie's Street Chic, consists largely of pictures of her trying out various fashion combinations and is considered an influential arbiter of teen style.

Some teen bloggers use their perspective to give more serious advice to their peers. For example, while Gurl.com covers a fair amount of the usual fashion and pop culture territory, it also features peer-to-peer advice about teen dating and health issues. Sites like that tap into the fact that sometimes teens feel more comfortable hearing about sensitive subjects from their peers than from people their parents' age. On the other hand, OneBridgeofHope.com gives advice from the perspective of both teens and parents, via a mother-and-daughter team of bloggers.

Personal knowledge and interests can translate into wildly popular blogs, as is the case with some gaming blogs. For example, the gaming site Kotaku.com draws an estimated ten million monthly visitors. It is estimated that 12 percent of gamers like to read reviews on at least a weekly basis.

A blog can also center around special expertise, by providing how-to tips on things like cooking or music. Video is a good idea for this type of blog, since often it is more effective to demonstrate a technique visually rather than just describe it.

Blogs work best when the personal enthusiasm and knowledge of the blogger shines through in the content.

Interest in sports and entertainment is often a basis for blogs, though there is a great deal of competition in these areas. One approach can be to narrow the focus to appeal to followers

Audience members often respond best to content produced by their peers, though a multi-generational approach can add perspective.

of a particular team, celebrity, or genre by providing a degree of detailed coverage die-hard fans crave and can't find in mainstream media.

One can think of blogging as a form of conversation. If a person is passionate about a subject, feels knowledgeable talking about it, and is frequently thinking of new things to say, then that person has already found a possible basis for a blog.

Chapter FOUR

Making It Pay

So far, the focus of this book has been to describe what goes into a blog: the structural components, the skill sets required, and the subject matter. Now it's time to address what a blogger can get out of it—how to make it pay.

The most direct way to get paid for blogging is to attract a big enough audience to support any of a variety of different advertising models. However there are other paths a person can take to make money—and possibly build a career—out of blogging. It helps to know what the possibilities are, so that even if the high-profile approach of starting a popular blog does not work out, the experience involved may be a valuable stepping-stone to a career.

DIFFERENT APPROACHES TO BLOGGING FOR MONEY

Blogging is still new enough that business models for monetizing a blog are in a state of rapid development. Some of the fundamental principles involved will be discussed in more detail later in this chapter. Before going down that path though, it is

worth noting that there are a couple of other possibilities for how blogging can lead to a career. These may be less visible than running a high-profile blog, but they are equally viable.

One is to be a hired gun—a paid blogger on someone else's site. While blogs started out as very individualistic exercises, they have increasingly developed into brands that are not associated with a single individual. Rather, they will hire a team of bloggers with the right subject knowledge and style to fit the brand. While being a hired blogger is not as great as starting one's own site, it can be a much more reliable source of income. It can also be a good fit for a person who just likes the writing element of blogging and does not want to deal with technical and promotional tasks.

Even if someone starts blogging as a hobby or for a school project, this can still be the first step toward working as a hired blogger. The idea is to build up a portfolio of links to professional-quality posts. Writing about a range of different subjects, and perhaps experimenting with a variety of different styles, can give a blogger a broader portfolio to choose from, so that when it comes time to apply for a job the blogger can pick and choose samples of work that fit well with the potential employer.

Working as a hired blogger can be a full-time job, which often has the advantage of including benefits like access to a health care plan. On the other hand, many hired bloggers work on a freelance basis, which gives them more independence and the possibility of working for a few different sites at once.

A hired blogger will generally have their own byline, but another career path comes from either ghostwriting for other people or writing more generic corporate content. In those cases, blogging is less about attracting an audience than it is about promoting products and encouraging customer loyalty. While working behind the scenes in this manner is not going to satisfy anyone seeking the visibility and freedom of expression generally associated with blogging, it can be a useful step toward gaining experience while also earning a steady paycheck.

REVENUE STREAMS

Bloggers who aspire to running their own sites should understand how to monetize their sites. Even those who write for others might find it useful to know how those sites make money. Again, business models for blogging are still evolving, so anyone serious

7 WEB BANNERS
STANDARD SIZES

LEADERBOARD (728x90)

SAMPLE TEXT
LOREM IPSUM DOLOR SIT AMET

Lorem ipsum dolor sit amet, consectetur adipiscing elit, sed do eiusmod tempor incid unt ut labe dolore ma aliqua, ut enim ad minim veniamqu.

SIGN UP NOW

WWW.WEBSITE.COM

SQUARE (336x280)

SAMPLE TEXT
LOREM IPSUM DOLOR SIT AMET

Lorem ipsum dolor sit amet, consectetur adipiscing elit, sed do eiusmod tempor incid unt ut labe dolore ma aliqua, ut enim ad minim veniamqu.

Lorem ipsum dolor sit amet, consectetur adipiscing elit, sed do eiusmod tem or incid

WWW.WEBSITE.COM

SIGN UP NOW

BUTTON (120x90)

SAMPLE TEXT
LOREM IPSUM DOLOR SIT AMET

SIGN UP NOW

WWW.WEBSITE.COM

BUTTON (120x60)

SAMPLE TEXT

SIGN UP NOW

SKYSCRAPER (160x600)

SAMPLE TEXT

Lorem ipsum dolor sit amet, consectetur adipiscing elit, sed do eiusmod tempor incid unt ut labe dolore ma aliqua, ut enim ad minim veniamqu.

Lorem ipsum dolor sit amet, consectetur adipiscing elit, sed do eiusmod tem or incid

Lorem ipsum dolor sit amet, consectetur adipiscing elit, sed do eiusmod tempor incid unt ut labe dolore ma aliqua, ut enim ad minim veniamqu.

Lorem ipsum dolor sit amet, consectetur adipiscing elit, sed do eiusmod tem or incid

SIGN UP NOW

WWW.WEBSITE.COM

SQUARE (250x250)

SAMPLE TEXT
LOREM IPSUM DOLOR SIT AMET

Lorem ipsum dolor sit amet, consectetur adipiscing elit, sed do eiusmod tempor incid unt ut labe dolore ma aliqua, ut enim ad minim veniamqu.

Lorem ipsum dolor sit amet, consectetur adipiscing elit, sed do eiusmod tem or incid

WWW.WEBSITE.COM

SIGN UP NOW

HALF BANNER (234x60)

SAMPLE TEXT

SIGN UP NOW

WWW.WEBSITE.COM

EPS 10

- 100% Editable EPS Vector Files
- Easy to Use
- Easy to Change Colors
- All Elements Are Grouped

Banner ads can occupy a variety of spaces in a screen layout, and are just one way of generating revenue from a blog.

about the business should check out sites related to the industry, such as eMarketer.com, to read about the latest approaches.

People who have grown up reading blogs are already very familiar with the most obvious forms of advertising. Banner ads are the simplest. These are the static blocks of ad copy that occupy a portion of a web page. Pop-up ads demand more attention—they tend to obscure the copy the reader was trying to look at. But they are increasingly being foiled by pop-up blockers. Another format is streaming video, which might appear on the front end of a content video or run on a portion of the screen for blogs with written content.

Those forms of advertising are highly visible, and as a result users often find them highly annoying. In response, bloggers have turned to less obtrusive forms of advertising, though these also have a controversial side to them.

Native advertising is content that fits the general style of the editorial content, but which is written to promote a particular product. Being content-based, this advertising is less disruptive to the user experience than more overt forms of advertising, but users sometimes resent when it is hard to distinguish between paid and editorial content.

Another possible revenue channel is to harvest data from visitors. This typically involves getting them to sign up for things, such as contests or subscription lists, which require them to share their email addresses and possibly other information which can be useful in ad targeting. This information can then be used for cross-channel marketing campaigns, such as using email to reach out to people who have registered with the blogging site. There is also a secondary market for selling user data to ad companies for their own use.

Commerce vs. Credibility

Banner ads, pop-ups, streaming video spots, native content, email blasts...

As described in this chapter, there are plenty of ways to capitalize on the popularity of a blogging site. However, the right balance has to be struck, because too much commercialization can undermine the credibility of a site.

These days, everyone expects to see ads on a site, but the problem comes when they are so prominent that they interfere with navigation of the site. Pop-ups are a particular nuisance in this regard. Also, given the prevalence of pop-up blockers, a revenue model that relies on this form of advertising might not be the most viable approach.

Other forms of advertising can also alienate an audience. Bloggers have to be very careful about native content, for example, because once people recognize that some posts were bought and paid for, it will lead them to question how genuine everything on the site is. Email blasts can be a way to get some extra revenue out of subscriber lists, but if they clog up people's in-boxes they will start to view being a subscriber as more trouble than it is worth.

Perhaps the best advice for any blogger contemplating a revenue model is to think about what the user experience is going to be like. Think about what it is like to visit a site

(continued on the next page)

(continued from the previous page)

that is overpopulated by tacky ads, is continually interrupted by pop-ups, or is loaded with content that seems to be shilling for a product rather than providing information or entertainment.

If commercialization starts getting in the way of enjoyment of the site, it is time to tone it down a bit before the audience starts getting turned off.

There are ethical debates about different advertising methods. For example, is it better to hit consumers over the head with an obvious ad, or market to them in more subtle ways without them realizing it? Each blogger might find a different balance between these approaches, but in any case, it is important to remember that in a sense, the user and the blogger need each other. The site visitor is getting to view content whose only price is having to view the occasional ad; the blogger needs site visitors in order to sell advertising without alienating the audience.

While any blogger could try to sell advertising directly, to reach a sufficient volume plus meet the increasingly complex targeting and measurement requirements of advertisers it may be best to work with an advertising network like Google's AdSense. Naturally, this means giving up a cut of the revenues, but that will probably be cheaper than trying to create an advertising infrastructure from scratch.

Of course, the key to getting attention from advertisers is to build a big audience. Techniques for doing that will be discussed in the upcoming section on building an audience.

BUILDING AN AUDIENCE

Making money from online advertising is a numbers game. The more people a site attracts, the more advertisers will pay. So, if you want to profit from blogging, building an audience is key. The following is a list of techniques to consider:

- **Networking.** Make sure that friends and family are aware of the blog, and reach out to teachers because they can help reach a much broader audience. Also, it helps to comment on related blogs and offer to exchange guest blog slots with other bloggers.

Getting friends and family to read and share blog posts is a grassroots way to get started with promoting a new site.

- **Subscription lists.** Once someone visits the site, the idea is to keep them coming back. Obviously, the quality of the content has something to do with that, but these days there is plenty of competition for people's attention. One way to keep a blog in front of the audience is to offer to let visitors sign up for a free subscription list. That allows for regular emails to this list with links to new posts, or perhaps to a weekly "best of the blog" compilation.

- **Really Simple Syndication (RSS).** These are links to news aggregators that let people sign up to get updates on their favorite blogs. Bloggers should be sure to have clearly-marked icons with each article to prompt viewers to select the site for inclusion in their user's RSS feeds.

As a blogging site gains popularity, fans will wait enthusiastically for new posts, and then share them with their friends.

- **Syndication.** Sites like the Huffington Post will carry quality blog posts from other sites. This often does not pay, but it is a great way to get exposure to a wider audience.

- **Search engine optimization (SEO).** This is a strategy for using keyword phrases that will help a post get a good ranking in search engine results. As with many aspects of blogging, this is an ever-evolving art: search engine algorithms are somewhat mysterious and are regularly tweaked. However, learning the rudiments of SEO is a good move for any blogger.

- **Linking strategies.** Linking to credible websites can help improve search engine rankings, though the real prize is getting quality back links. This means having popular sites link to your blog, which is yet another reason to maintain an active networking effort.

- **User engagement.** Contests and opinion polls are ways of getting people to interact with a site, which helps keep people interested. Even something as simple as encouraging comments on posts can help.

- **Social media teasing.** Sharing links and pictures on social media sites such as Facebook, Twitter, Snapchat, and Instagram is a good way to show people teasers, little snippets of information, about interesting posts to draw them to the blog.

- **Press outreach.** Bloggers with special areas of expertise can be valuable sources for reporters. A blogger should try to leverage any insider knowledge of a particular field, polling data, or proprietary statistical analysis by reaching out to reporters who cover related topics.

Building an audience tends to have a snowballing effect. Momentum starts slowly, but if people like what you do, all of a sudden you'll have more and more people out there reposting your articles. Effectively, at that point, dedicated fans of the site will do much of the promotional work for you. However, it will never get to that point if you don't make the effort to get the snowball rolling.

Chapter FIVE

Tomorrow's Blog: Challenges and Opportunities

Newspapers date back to colonial times, and radio broadcasts have been going on for over a hundred years. Even television broadcasting is approaching its one hundredth birthday.

Blogging, on the other hand, is very much a twenty-first-century phenomenon. That is part of what makes it so dynamic and exciting, but also so challenging. Anyone who is serious about blogging needs to be committed to keeping pace with the changes.

THE CHANGING FACE OF BLOGGING

Visually, the earliest blogs had more in common with a piece of typewritten paper than with today's website formats. The face of blogging has become more colorful, more varied, and more engaging.

Actually, blogs have to be prepared to have multiple faces. A web page that is formatted for a laptop will not display well on a tablet, let alone on a smartphone. Having the format fit the device makes blogs more accessible for their users, but it also raises the technical bar for setting up and maintaining a blog site.

Each of the faces a blog takes on for various devices has to be more varied than in the past. While once vlogging was a completely distinct subset of blogging, even blogs that rely primarily on the written word are increasingly incorporating video clips. In all cases, whether in print format or on video, the ability to combine words and pictures to tell a story is also becoming the standard for how blogs are presented. It is how the audience expects to consume its information and entertainment.

A key example of the words-and-picture approach is the infographic. These are especially valuable for telling a story with quantitative data. Put a table full of statistics on a page and people's eyes tend to glaze over. Lead them through those same statistics with artwork and succinct commentary, and they will have a much better chance of getting the point. Infographics are also very popular with journalists, so they can be a great way for a blogger to get content picked up by other blogs and publications.

VIDEO ELEMENTS

As noted above, video is increasingly being incorporated into written-word blogs, but simply streaming some video content is not enough to make a blog seem thoroughly professional and contemporary. The nature of the video content being posted is also rapidly evolving.

Will Complexity Make Blogging Less Democratic?

Whether it is the visual face of blogs or the business methods behind them, one trend is pervasive — the game is getting more complicated.

Blogging once meant nothing more than sitting down at the computer keyboard now and then and writing some interesting thoughts. Today's blogger is expected to put together a compelling mix of videos, graphics, and text presented in formats suitable for multiple devices while checking the latest metrics to see how the site's programmatic advertising campaigns are going — and, of course, a blogger must regularly come up with something interesting to say on the blog.

Blogging is still very democratic in the sense that in theory, anyone who is reasonably computer literate can do it. However, meeting the standard currently being set by blogs requires a much broader set of skills and a greater degree of time and effort. Just about anyone can still do it, but not just anyone can be competitive.

To some extent, the increasing complexity of blogging can be seen as finding a happy medium. While it might make it tougher to compete for attention, it also raises content standards. Meanwhile, the numbers make one thing clear: the increased complexity of blogging is not winnowing down the number of blogs. Blogging is still very democratic, but higher standards might just make it a little easier to spot which of the many voices out there should be taken seriously.

Initially, many bloggers' idea of incorporating video was simply to sit in front of a web cam talking. Now video production techniques being used have gotten much more sophisticated, but the evolution of video in blogging goes beyond how well-produced the videos are. An even more significant change is in what role those videos are playing.

After all, a talking head shot really conveys little more information than a written blog would, except letting the viewers know whether or not the blogger has washed his hair that day or what kind of sweaters she likes. The real point of adding video should be to accomplish things that simply printing words cannot, and bloggers are increasingly rising to this challenge.

For example, a clip from broadcast footage of a sporting or news event may be shown to kick off a discussion of what happened. In this way, the blogger is not just using video to help illustrate a point, but is also acting as a curator, finding and directing people toward interesting clips they might otherwise have missed.

Thanks to smartphones, there are now cameras on the scene almost everywhere, and this form of eyewitness reporting has also become a vital part of blogging. In the 1960s, antiwar protesters at the Democratic National Convention in Chicago chanted "the whole world is watching," but the truth is that the world was watching only as long as the network television cameras were rolling. With the prevalence of smartphones, now the whole world really is watching virtually all the time whether it is antigovernment protesters in Egypt, a traffic stop in the United States, or just something cute your cat did last night.

Smartphone cameras are one element in the importance of eyewitness footage, but without blogs most of that footage would reach a very limited audience. The incorporation of that footage into blogs is what helps it spread around the world.

Another way that the role of video in blogging is rapidly changing is that created content has joined commentary and reportage as material that has an online mass audience. Vloggers now produce skits and other fictional content that have regular audiences on YouTube channels numbering in the millions.

The first generation of bloggers can be thought of as having sidestepped traditional newspaper editors to get their content directly in front of people. Now, created video content is allowing vloggers to sidestep entertainment industry executives and let the audience decide what they want to watch.

A variety of analytics are available to help bloggers improve their search rankings through SEO techniques, determine causes for increased or decreased traffic, and other tasks.

EVOLVING BUSINESS ISSUES

Some of the increased complexity of blogs is visible, but at least as much goes on behind the scenes in terms of the business of blogging.

SEO, for example, has taken on the intensity of a world-class competitive sport. Trying to write copy that will garner a favorable ranking in online searches on related topics may once have merely been about relevance, but once people realized just how valuable those first-page rankings were, it became a twenty-four-hour-a-day global pursuit.

Some of the early techniques—simply stuffing copy full of key search phrases, or repeatedly republishing the same copy to generate volume—did not result in quality content. As a result, search engines like Google are constantly tweaking their algorithms to reward quality over purely

Automated ad targeting tools can allow a site to match ads with selected segments of its audience, to better appeal to advertisers.

fraudulent attempts at exploitation. This means in turn that even bloggers focused on quality must regularly adjust their policies so their efforts are rewarded rather than punished by new search criteria.

Online advertising is another area of rapid change. When blogs first became popular, advertisers somewhat blindly threw money at them, but no longer. There is an increased emphasis on metrics that can demonstrate the results of any advertising campaign.

Simply knowing the number of visitors to a website is not enough. Advertisers now want to know how many people viewed the part of the screen where their ad is placed, how much of the ad was visible in the area the viewer had scrolled to, and how long that visitor stayed there.

One other important detail about those ad views: they had better have been viewed by an actual human. The incentives involved in scoring a big audience for advertisers led to a boom in ad fraud, using automated "bots" to visit pages and beef up apparent ad views. In response, advertising networks are deploying their own programs using behavioral analysis to distinguish real from digital ad viewers.

Speaking of ad networks, these middlemen who match advertisers with appropriate inventory of advertising space are playing an ever-growing role. Not only can they bring to the table a critical mass that few blogs or advertisers would represent on their own, but they have the technological capability to meet the increasingly complex demands of advertisers.

Advertisers want to target certain audience segments, and they want to place those ads in front of those segments as cost efficiently as possible. To accomplish this, sophisticated advertisers use programmatic ad buying, which can automatically scour an ad network's inventory of available ad space to find placements that will match an advertiser's target segments at the most attractive cost relative to the size of the viewership. Programmatic ad buying is a far cry from negotiating ads person to person, one at a time, and ad networks are essential for facilitating it.

Finally, another evolving business angle any would-be blogger should be aware of is legal liability. Specifically, there are two major issues that can get a blog sued for its content: libel and plagiarism.

In the online world, people are used to being able to take shots at celebrities, athletes, or products, but as a blog grows in popularity it also faces a higher level of responsibility to have a basis for any derogatory statements it makes. Otherwise it could face a lawsuit for libel, which is the publication of false and defamatory statements.

Plagiarism is also a tricky issue given the nature of blogging. Blogs are a platform for passing along interesting facts and materials from other sources, but simply copying someone else's material can lead to a plagiarism suit. Posting video clips is also popular, but can also be a copyright violation. The best advice is to always attribute the source when citing a fact or quote from somewhere else, and if you are posting extended portions of someone else's material, get permission.

Remember, the more successful blogging becomes as a business, the more prone it will be to legal disputes.

A REWARDING HOBBY AND CAREER

Blogging is a great hobby because it can teach so many valuable skills—writing, performing, video production, and marketing.

> Blogging can open up a channel of mass communication and business opportunity that is accessible to young people with ambitious ideas.

Besides the variety of careers that blogging can lead to directly, those skills should be valuable no matter what career you pursue.

Perhaps the greatest thing about blogging, though, is that it is a platform so completely open to young people. The barrier to entry is low, and unlike many occupations, youth is actually an advantage rather than a drawback. Fresh voices and youthful perspectives are valued rather than viewed as evidence of inexperience.

In fact, because the rules are changing all the time, experience is of limited value. The technology, style, and business models of blogging are a moving target. New entrants can quickly understand the rules of blogging as well as old hands and even help to shape those rules.

Ultimately, whether blogging proves to be just a short-term hobby or a long-term career path for you, remember that amateurs and professionals alike have their reputations on the line when they write a blog post or create a video. Knowing that should help inspire your best work, and there is no telling how many people you might eventually reach with that work.

Glossary

aggregator A website or application that assembles content from multiple sources rather than just presenting content from one source.

banner ads An advertisement displayed across a designated block of space on a web page.

B2B marketing Marketing targeted from one business to another business, rather than to retail customers.

business model The planned methods an enterprise has for growing its revenue base and earning a profit.

byline A line usually displayed under the title of an article that shows and describes who wrote the article.

digital footprint The online record a person leaves behind consisting of things he or she has posted over time.

evergreen content Website material which is intended to have lasting relevance, rather than relate specifically to recent events.

ghostwriting Writing for another person for a publication under that person's name rather than the writer's own.

keyword phrase A word or group of words likely to be used in search inquiries on a given topic; effective use of such expressions can improve an article's ranking in search results.

monetize To utilize a site's popularity to generate revenue streams through means such as advertising.

native advertising Paid promotional content which has the look and style of the editorial content and thus may not be immediately recognized to be an advertisement.

niche audience An audience that is interested in content that caters to a specific interest and/or personality rather than to a general or diverse set of topics or voices.

peer-to-peer community Groups of people with similar interests who share insights and advice on a topic on which they aren't necessarily experts.

platform The technological base from which a website is launched and maintained.

pop-up ads Advertisements that appear over the content the user intended to view, and sometimes take some action by the user to make disappear.

programmatic advertising The use of automation to buy advertising more efficiently.

search engine optimization (SEO) The tailoring of online content to achieve favorable rankings in searches relevant to that content.

self-hosted website A website that provides and controls its own platform, as opposed to relying on a third-party platform.

site housekeeping Various tasks involved in keeping a site up-to-date, such as deleting outdated content, reformatting, and fixing bugs.

traffic In an online context, this is the volume of users that visit a site and how frequently they return.

For More Information

BlogsCanada.ca

Website: http://blogscanada.ca

This is a compilation of the best and most popular Canadian blogs, offering a subscription service that helps Canadians locate blogs with a local emphasis.

eMarketer

11 Times Square

New York, NY 10036

Website: http://www.emarketer.com

This news and research organization provides insights into digital marketing trends for content providers and advertisers.

Freelancer.com

Level 20, World Square

680 George Street

Sydney, New South Wales

Australia 2000

Email: support@freelancer.com

Website: https://www.freelancer.com

This is the world's largest freelancing exchange, matching freelance writers, designers, online publishers, and other talent with employers.

International Bloggers' Association

PO Box 193

Elizabethtown, KY 42702

Website: http://www.internationalbloggersassociation.com

This organization is dedicated to helping bloggers succeed and to creating a supportive community of bloggers.

Kids' Blog Club

Email: joanne@kidsblogclub.com

Website: http://kidsblogclub.com

This site highlights kids' blogs and provides guidance and support for kid bloggers and their parents.

National Association of Independent Writers and Editors

PO Box 549

Ashland, VA 23005

Website: http://naiwe.com

This professional association provides platform support for bloggers as well as online publishing tools and tips.

Top Blogs: Canada's Best Blogs

URL: http://topblogs.ca/

This list of Canada's top blogs is ranked by daily page views. It is a platform bloggers can join to seek greater exposure.

WEBSITES

Because of the changing nature of internet links, Rosen Publishing has developed an online list of websites related to the subject of this book. This site is updated regularly. Please use this link to access this list:

For Further Reading

Bodnar, Jacqueline. *Starting Your Career as a Professional Blogger.* New York, NY: Allworth Press, 2013.

Brown, Tracy. *Blogger or Journalist? Evaluating What Is Press in the Digital Age.* New York, NY: Rosen Central, 2012.

Charlesworth, Alan. *Digital Marketing: A Practical Approach.* New York, NY: Routledge, 2014.

Clarkson, Stephanie. *Vlog It!* New York, NY: Scholastic, 2015.

Dawson, Shane. *I Hate My Selfie: A Collection of Essays by Shane Dawson.* New York, NY: Atria Books, 2015.

Foust, James C., Edward J. Fink, and Lynne S. Gross. *Video Production: Disciplines and Techniques.* Scottsdale, AZ: Holcomb Hathaway, 2012.

Handley, Ann, and C. C. Chapman. *Content Rules: How to Create Killer Blogs, Podcasts, Videos, Ebooks, Webinars (and More) that Engage Customers and Ignite Your Business.* Hoboken, NJ: John Wiley & Sons, Inc., 2012.

Handley, Ann. *Everybody Writes: Your Go-To Guide to Creating Ridiculously Good Content.* Hoboken, NJ: Wiley, 2014.

Holiday, Ryan. *Growth Hacker Marketing: A Primer on the Future of PR, Marketing, and Advertising.* New York, NY: Portfolio/Penguin, 2014.

Houghton, Robin. *Blogging for Creatives: How designers, artists, crafters, and writers can blog to make contacts, win business, and build success.* Blue Ash, OH: F+W Media, 2012.

James-Enger, Kelly. *Writer for Hire: 101 Secrets to Freelance Success.* Blue Ash, OH: F+W Media, 2012.

Keller, Jessalynn. *Girls' Feminist Blogging in a Postfeminist Age.* New York, NY: Routledge, 2015.

Manriquez, Antonio, and Thomas McCluskey. *Video Production 101.* San Francisco, CA: Peachpit Press, 2015.

McAllister, Jenn. *Really Professional Internet Person.* New York, NY: Scholastic, 2015.

Petit, Zachary. *Freelance Writing: How to Write, Work, & Thrive On Your Own Terms.* Blue Ash, OH: F+W Media, 2015.

Pullman, George. *Writing Online: Rhetoric for the Digital Age.* Indianapolis, IN: Hackett Publishing Company, Inc., 2016.

Saleh, Naveed. *The Complete Guide to Article Writing: How to Write Successful Articles for Online and Print Markets.* Blue Ash, OH: F+W Media, 2013.

Scott, David Meerman. *The New Rules of Marketing and PR: How to Use Social Media, Online Video, Applications, Blogs, News Releases & Viral Marketing to Reach Buyers Directly.* Hoboken, NY: Wiley, 2015.

Sugg, Zoe. *Girl Online: The First Novel by Zoella.* New York, NY: Atria Books, 2014.

Walter, Ekaterina, and Jessica Gioglio. *The Power of Visual Storytelling: How to Use Visuals, Videos, and Social Media to Market Your Brand.* New York, NY: McGraw Hill Education, 2014.

Bibliography

Baker, Dillon. "Is it Plagiarism? (a flowchart)" The Freelancer. February 16, 2016 (http://contently.net/2016/02/16/resources/ flowchart-will-save-plagiarizing/?utm_source=TF -newsletter&utm_medium=email&utm_campaign =plagiarism-flowchart).

"Blog Posts Written Today." Worldometers. Retrieved March 8, 2016 (http://www.worldometers.info/blogs/).

Bump, Philip. "Finally, We Know how Many Bloggers Live in Their Parents' Basement." *Washington Post*, March 25, 2015.

Butow, Eric, and Rebecca Bollwitt. *Blogging to Drive Business.* Indianapolis, IN: Que Publishing, 2010.

Cho, Joy Deangdeelert. *Blog Inc.: Blogging for Passion, Profit, and to Create Community.* San Francisco, CA: Chronicle Books, 2012.

Goldring, Emily. "Top 50 Gaming Blogs." Soomla. February 29, 2016 (http://blog.soom.la/2016/02/top-gaming-blogs.html).

Gutman, Allison. "Teen Scene: The New Wave of Young Fashion Bloggers." Guest of a Guest, November 5, 2014 (http://guestofaguest.com/blogosphere/teen-scene-the -new-wave-of-young-fashion-bloggers).

Handley, Ann, and C.C. Chapman. *Content Rules.* Hoboken, NJ: John Wiley & Sons, Inc., 2012.

Jacobs, Harrison. "The Richest YouTube Stars." Business Insider, March 10, 2014 (http://www.businessinsider.com/ richest-youtube-stars-2014-3).

Knorr, Caroline. "10 YouTube Stars Your Kids Love." Common Sense Media, September 4, 2014 (https://www. commonsensemedia.org/ blog/10-youtube-stars-your-kids-love).

Marshall, Jack. "WTF is Programmatic Advertising?" Digiday, February 20, 2014 (http://digiday.com/platforms/what-is

-programmatic-advertising/).

Reed, Jon. *Get Up to Speed with Online Marketing.* Upper Saddle River, NJ: Pearson Education, 2012.

Schaefer, Mark W. and Stanford A.Smith. *Born to Blog.* New York, NY: McGraw Hill Education, 2013.

Simone, Seleah. "Teen Dream: The Top Bloggers Under 18." Guest of a Guest, January 12, 2012 (http://guestofaguest.com/blogosphere/ teen-dream-the-top-10-bloggers-under-18).

Swartz, John. "During Viewability Growing Pains, Let's Agree to Agree." Technorati, January 27, 2015 (http://technorati.com/ during-viewability-growing-pains-lets-agree-to-agree/).

Swartz, John. "The Futures of Programmatic Retargeting, Measurement and Video." Technorati, October 24, 2014 (http://technorati.com/ the-futures-of-programmatic-retargeting-measurement-and- video/).

"Top 15 Most Popular Blogs." eBiz MBA Guide. Retrieved February 16, 2016 (http://www.ebizmba.com/articles/blogs).

"Top Seller Rankings in Programmatic Advertising." Pixalate. Retrieved February 18, 2016 (http://www.pixalate.com/sellertrustindex/#!global).

"What Stops Marketers from Deriving Value from Data-Driven Efforts." eMarketer, February 18, 2016 (http://www.emarketer.com/Article/ What-Stops-Marketers-Deriving-Value-Data-Driven- Efforts/1013600?ecid=NL1001).

White, Charlie, and John Biggs. *Bloggers Boot Camp.* Waltham, MA: Focal Press, 2012.

Index

A

B

C

D

E

ABOUT THE AUTHOR

With his varied background, Richard Barrington is an example of the ingredients that make up a successful blogger. His three decades of financial industry experience give him a specialized area of expertise, to which he adds the communication skills of a professional writer who has authored books and online material for a variety of publishers. Barrington has been blogging regularly since 2007, and has had material syndicated on MSN.com, the Huffington Post, and Forbes.com. He has also appeared on National Public Radio's *Talk of the Nation*, American Public Media's *Marketplace*, and Fox Business News. He graduated from St. John Fisher College with a BA in communications, and earned his chartered financial analyst designation from the CFA Institute.

PHOTO CREDITS